ABORIGINAL BIOGRAPHIES

Musicians

KAITE GOLDSWORTHY

Weigl

Published by Weigl Educational Publishers Limited
6325 10th Street SE
Calgary, Alberta T2H 2Z9
Website: www.weigl.ca

Library and Archives Canada Cataloguing in Publication

Goldsworthy, Kaite
     Musicians / Kaite Goldsworthy.
(Canadian Aboriginal biographies)
Includes index.
ISBN 978-1-77071-456-4 (bound).—ISBN 978-1-77071-460-1 (pbk.)

     1. Indian musicians—Canada—Biography—Juvenile literature.
2. Native musicians—Canada—Biography—Juvenile literature.
3. Indians of North America—Canada—Music—History and
criticism—Juvenile literature. I. Title. II. Series: Canadian
Aboriginal biographies

ML3929.G624 2012   j780.92'397   C2011-908196-2

Printed in the United States of America in North Mankato, Minnesota
1 2 3 4 5 6 7 8 9 0 16 15 14 13 12

082012
WEP250612

Senior Editor: Heather Kissock
Art Director: Terry Paulhus

We gratefully acknowledge the financial support of the Government of Canada through the Canada Book Fund for our publishing activities.

CONTENTS

22

10

14

Introduction

Canada is home to many talented **Aboriginal** musicians who work in many different styles of music, including country, folk, rock, pop, and **blues**. They are singers and songwriters, telling stories in their works and sharing their views of the world through their **lyrics**. These musicians play a variety of instruments, including guitar, piano, and drums. They have won many awards, both at home and around the world. Aboriginal musicians have also played for all kinds of audiences, from everyday people to royalty.

Aboriginal Canadians include First Nations, Inuit, and **Métis**. Many Aboriginal cultures do not have a separate word to describe music. It is just a part of their everyday life. Traditionally, there were two types of Aboriginal music. They were social music, often accompanied by dancing, and ceremonial music. Social music was for community celebrations and was for everyone to enjoy.

TANYA TAGAQ

Ceremonial music was more spiritual. It was reserved for special ceremonies such as sun dances.

Traditionally, Aboriginal people made music using such instruments as drums, rattles, and flutes. They also often made music using just their voices. Many Aboriginal Canadian musicians today are proud of their heritage and are influenced by the music of their **ancestors**. To express their pride, they often use Aboriginal traditions and themes in their music and lyrics. This way, their music lets them stay connected to their past.

Some Aboriginal musicians, such as Robbie Robertson and Tom Jackson, have had widespread success. Others, including Susan Aglukark, Derek Miller, and Shane Yellowbird, are getting more attention and recognition every day. Some musicians, such as Tanya Tagaq, practice a type of music that many people do not know about. With pride in their heritage, these artists are paving the way for the success of other Aboriginal musicians.

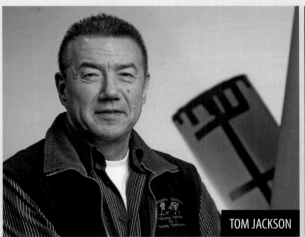
TOM JACKSON

DEREK MILLER

SUSAN AGLUKARK

ROBBIE ROBERTSON

SHANE YELLOWBIRD

Guitarist, Singer, and Songwriter
Robbie Robertson

Robbie Robertson is one of the most successful Canadian Aboriginal musicians in North America. Best known as the guitar player and songwriter for The Band, he has worked with some of the biggest stars in music, such as Eric Clapton, Bob Dylan, and Nelly Furtado. Robertson has won several music awards, including **Grammy Awards** and **Juno Awards**. His other achievements include membership in the Canadian Music Hall of Fame and Canadian Songwriters Hall of Fame, as well as in the Rock and Roll Hall of Fame.

Many of Robertson's solo albums explore his Aboriginal and **Mohawk** roots. These albums

Personal Profile

In 2011, *Rolling Stone* magazine placed Robertson on its list of 100 Greatest Guitarists.

include *Robbie Robertson, Storyville, Music for the Native Americans,* and *Contact from the Underworld of Redboy.* Robertson's songs have helped bring wider attention to Aboriginal music.

Early Years

Jaime Robbie Klegerman was born in 1943 in Toronto, where he grew up. His father, Alexander, died when Robbie was very young. His mother, Rosemarie, married James Robertson. When Robertson adopted Robbie, Robbie took his stepfather's last name.

Rosemarie was a Mohawk. She had been raised on the Six Nations **reserve** near Brantford, Ontario. Every summer, she took her son to the reserve to visit relatives. Robertson received his first guitar on the reserve. He learned how to play from his relatives.

> **"***I remember from my earliest years, . . . people speaking . . . in a certain kind of rhythm and telling stories and sharing experiences in a way that was different in Indian country than it was other places. And I was really struck by this and obviously very affected by it, because it's always come out in my songs.***"**

Robertson was born and raised in Toronto, the largest city in Canada and a key player in the Canadian music industry. Many record labels have offices in Toronto, and the city is known for its vibrant music scene.

BORN Jaime Robbie Robertson was born on July 5, 1943, in Toronto, Ontario.

FAMILY Robertson was raised by his mother, a Mohawk. He married journalist Dominique Bourgeois in 1967. They later divorced. The couple has two daughters, Alexandra and Delphine, and a son, Sebastian.

EDUCATION Robertson has an honorary degree from Queen's University in Kingston, Ontario.

CAREER He is a record producer as well as a singer, songwriter, and guitarist. Robertson has won many awards for his music. He has also acted and worked on the music for movies.

"It all added up to something that's making me feel proud."

Developing Skills

As a teenager, Robertson devoted much of his spare time to playing the guitar. He practised daily and jammed with his friends. He also began writing songs. Music became his focus, and he left high school before graduating to become a part of the local music scene.

Robertson played guitar in a series of rock and roll bands. Among them were Robbie Robertson and the Rhythm Chords, Thumper and the Trambones, and Robbie and the Robots. As they played in clubs around Toronto, Robertson became known as a talented guitarist.

Members of The Band included Levon Helm, Garth Hudson, Robbie Robertson, Rick Danko, and Richard Manuel.

The Path to Success

Robertson worked hard on his music, but he struggled to find band members who had the same dedication he had. His big break came in 1960, when Canadian singer Ronnie Hawkins recorded two songs that Robertson had written. Then, Hawkins asked Robertson to join his backing band, the Hawks. Robertson became the lead guitarist. Hawkins and the Hawks toured around Canada and the United States.

In 1964, Robertson and the other members of the Hawks left Hawkins and formed their own band, which they called the Canadian Squires. In 1967, the group's name became The Band. They released several albums, including *Music From Big Pink*. "The Weight," which was written by Robertson and became one of The Band's best-known songs, is on that album. Robertson also wrote many of The Band's other popular songs, such as "The Night They Drove Old Dixie Down."

Robertson and The Band were extremely successful in the 1960s and 1970s, but the rock and roll lifestyle was hard. The Band went on tour often and spent a great deal of time away from their families. Eventually, Robertson grew tired of touring. In 1976, The Band decided to break up. They performed a final concert, called "The Last Waltz," which was filmed as a documentary.

Robertson went on to work on **soundtracks** for films. Then, in 1987, he released *Robbie Robertson*, his first solo album. In 1994, he began to get in touch with his Mohawk heritage, recording an album called *Music for the Native Americans*. One of the songs on the album, "Heartbeat Drum Song," became a hit. He performed it at a concert in Italy that celebrated Native American music. Robertson is still making recordings today. Throughout his career, he has never forgotten his Aboriginal history, which he describes as a great source of pride.

Accomplishments

1989 Robertson wins three awards for his first solo album, *Robbie Robertson*, at the Juno Awards. They are Album of the Year, Producer of the Year, and Male Vocalist of the Year. Also, The Band is inducted into the Juno Hall of Fame.

1994 The Band is inducted into the Rock and Roll Hall of Fame.

2003 Robertson receives the National Aboriginal Achievement Award for Lifetime Achievement.

2008 The Band receives the Grammy Lifetime Achievement Award.

2011 Robertson is inducted into the Canadian Songwriters Hall of Fame and receives the **Order of Canada**.

Singer, Songwriter, Actor, and Activist
Tom Jackson

Tom Jackson is one of Canada's most respected and talented Aboriginal entertainers. He is a singer, songwriter, actor, and **activist** who overcame great challenges to become an example to many people, especially Aboriginal youth. Throughout his career, he has used his unique gift of song to bring people together for many worthy causes. Jackson has appeared in many films and TV shows, but music is his first and greatest love. He has recorded many albums and has toured Canada numerous times. He has also been nominated for Juno Awards.

Early Years
Tom Jackson was born on the One Arrow reserve in Saskatchewan in 1948. He is Métis. His mother, Rose Manymoon, was Cree, and his father, Marshall,

Jackson has helped organize many charitable events, such as a food collection event called The Holiday Train and a benefit concert for victims of the 2011 fire in Slave Lake, Alberta.

Personal Profile

was British. Jackson was the younger of two children. He has a sister named Marlene.

Jackson was raised in a loving home. However, the family moved around quite often. From an early age, Jackson learned to adapt to change. When he was seven, the

"You don't have to change the whole world, you just have to change your world, and the rest will follow."

family settled in Namao, Alberta, a small town north of Edmonton. There, something happened that would change his life forever.

Jackson has appeared on several TV shows, including *Star Trek*, *Law and Order*, and *Sesame Street*. He is also a star of *The Longhouse Tales*, a children's show based on traditional Aboriginal characters and mythology.

BORN Thomas Dale Jackson was born on October 27, 1948, on the One Arrow reserve in Saskatchewan.

FAMILY Jackson was raised by his parents, Rose and Marshall. He and his wife, Alison, have four children.

EDUCATION He has received honorary degrees from many Canadian universities.

CAREER In addition to being a singer and songwriter, Jackson worked as a radio and television producer. He is also a well-known TV and film actor.

Developing Skills

When he was 10, Jackson's parents gave him a guitar. It was the start of something magical. He loved playing, and he practised every day. Soon, he was playing along to songs on the radio and performing for friends and family.

Jackson hosted the Huron Carole Benefit Concert Series in 2000. This series has raised more than $2.5 million for food banks across Canada.

The Path to Success

Jackson and his family moved again when he was 14, this time to Winnipeg, Manitoba. Jackson had a hard time there. He struggled to find focus in his life. When he was 15, he dropped out of school. Not long after that, he ran away from home and spent the next seven years living on the streets of Winnipeg. It was there that his real understanding of **social issues** began.

Jackson experienced what it was like to be without a home or food. Despite these challenges, he never gave up. He worked hard to turn his life around and never lost sight of his hopes and dreams. To earn money, he began performing in coffee houses. He became popular and realized that he could inspire people through his music. Jackson began to work as a radio disc jockey. He also began recording albums and touring. His acting career began to flourish as well, and he starred on the hit Canadian TV show *North of 60* in the 1990s. The show was about Aboriginal people living in a town in northern Canada.

In 1996, a young actor on *North of 60* took his own life. This inspired Jackson to launch his Dreamcatcher Tour to bring attention to the problem of suicide in Aboriginal communities. For many years, he also starred in the Huron Carole Benefit Concert Series, a series of concerts held around Canada each Christmas to raise money for food banks. After the series ended, Jackson did a group of concerts called "Singing for Supper." He has also raised money with the "Swinging for Supper" tours. On these tours, he performs a concert and then plays golf with people. These concerts and tours have raised millions of dollars for Canadian food banks, disaster relief, and Canadian agencies that help young people who are having problems.

Accomplishments

1996 Jackson receives the National Aboriginal Achievement Award.

2000 He receives the Order of Canada.

2002 Jackson is awarded the Queen's Jubilee Medal.

2005 Jackson receives Centennial Medals from the provinces of Alberta and Saskatchewan.

2007 At the Juno Awards, Jackson is honoured with the Humanitarian Award for his work with the homeless and other less-fortunate people in Canada. He also receives the Humanitarian Award from the Academy of Canadian Cinema and Television.

2009 Jackson becomes the **chancellor** of Trent University, located in Peterborough, Ontario.

Folk and Pop Singer
Susan Aglukark

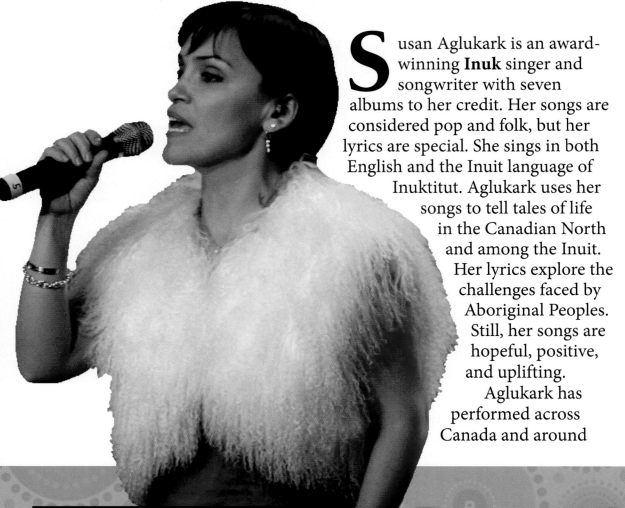

Susan Aglukark is an award-winning **Inuk** singer and songwriter with seven albums to her credit. Her songs are considered pop and folk, but her lyrics are special. She sings in both English and the Inuit language of Inuktitut. Aglukark uses her songs to tell tales of life in the Canadian North and among the Inuit. Her lyrics explore the challenges faced by Aboriginal Peoples. Still, her songs are hopeful, positive, and uplifting. Aglukark has performed across Canada and around

Aglukark has performed across Canada, including multiple appearances at the Canadian Aboriginal Music Awards. She has also performed around the world at festivals as far away as Sweden and Australia.

Personal Profile

the world. She has sung for Queen Elizabeth II and for President Jacques Chirac of France. She has also sung for Canadian prime ministers Jean Chretien and Brian Mulroney. Aglukark is an activist for Aboriginal rights. She has worked to raise political and social awareness of the issues facing Aboriginal Canadians. In addition, she is a popular **motivational speaker**.

Early Years

Susan Aglukark was born in 1967 in Manitoba. Her Inuit name is Uuliniq. Her family moved around a great deal during the first 12 years of her life. They eventually settled in Arviat in the Northwest Territories, which is now part of Nunavut. Aglukark's father was a minister, so she grew up singing hymns. Music was always part of her life, and Aglukark often sang in the church choir.

When she was quite young, Aglukark was abused by a family member. She later found out that he had also abused other children. She testified against him in court when he went on trial for hurting one of those other children.

Aglukark sings and speaks candidly about being part of the Canadian Aboriginal community and about the challenges Aboriginal peoples face.

BORN Susan Aglukark was born on January 27, 1967, in Churchill, Manitoba.

FAMILY Aglukark was raised by her parents, with her four sisters and two brothers. Aglukark is married. She and her husband, Jacques, have a son, Cameron.

EDUCATION Aglukark has received a number of honorary degrees from Canadian universities.

CAREER Aglukark worked as a **linguist** for the government and for a group that helps the Inuit. She is now a singer, songwriter, activist, and motivational speaker.

Developing Skills

While attending bible camp as a teenager, Aglukark learned to play the guitar. Music continued to be an important part of her life and her personal identity. Aglukark went to a number of different schools in the North. During her teenage years, she also found another outlet for her creativity when she began to write

"I have never considered myself a performer-singer. I'm a storyteller-singer more than anything."

poetry. Aglukark began to keep a journal as well.

In the early 1990s, Aglukark moved to Ottawa to work as a linguist and interpreter for the government in the Department of Indian and Northern Affairs. She also began writing songs at this time. After a year in Ottawa, Aglukark returned to northern Canada to work for the Inuit Tapirisat of Canada, an organisation that helps Inuit people.

Aglukark began singing publicly for people in the community. She was a popular performer, and word of her talent quickly spread. People at the Canadian Broadcasting Corporation (CBC) were impressed by her music.

They included her on an album featuring Arctic musicians.

The Path to Success

In 1992, Aglukark released her first album, *Arctic Rose*, independently, without having signed a **contract** with a record company. The album sold mostly in the Northwest Territories. When Aglukark became better known, she was offered a record contract and was able to leave her job with the Inuit Tapirisat. *Arctic Rose* was released again, this time across Canada, and it won a Juno Award in 1995.

Aglukark's 1995 album, *This Child*, contained her biggest hit song, "O Siem." "O Siem" means to welcome and honour guests. The song explores the idea that all people are really the same and should respect and honour one another.

This Child made Aglukark well known, but she found it hard to deal with success. She said she was a very private person and was uncomfortable with the attention she got. In time, however, she decided that she did want to sing, make recordings, and help young Aboriginals.

Since the mid-1990s, Aglukark has released several more albums and has had other hit songs. She has also received other honours and awards, including a Juno Award in 2000 for her

Aglukark has won three Juno awards during her career. Her first was awarded in 1995.

album *Big Feeling*. Aglukark continues to tour and perform, from small villages in Canada's North to stages around the world.

She is dedicated to her work as a motivational speaker and activist for Aboriginal people. Aglukark often talks about the problems of abuse and suicide. Several of her cousins committed suicide. She speaks about the need to build feelings of confidence and self-esteem, and she continues to inspire others with her voice and her message.

Accomplishments

1994 Aglukark wins the first National Aboriginal Achievement Award.

1995 She wins a Juno Award for Best New Solo Artist, and *Arctic Rose* wins for Best Music of Aboriginal Canada. Aglukark also receives an award from the Society of Composers, Authors and Music Publishers of Canada for "O Siem."

2000 The album *Big Feeling* wins a Juno Award for Aboriginal Recording of the Year.

2005 She is awarded the Order of Canada for her music and her work with the Aboriginal community.

2008 Aglukark is appointed Distinguished Scholar in Residence at the University of Alberta.

2012 Aglukark receives the Diamond Jubilee Medal for her achievements and contributions to Canada.

Singer, Songwriter, and Blues Guitarist
Derek Miller

Derek Miller is an Aboriginal guitarist, singer, and songwriter, known for his rock and blues style of music. He is also known for his skills as a guitar player. Miller describes his music as "Hillbilly soul with some Mohawk swagger." He has won many awards for his music and has worked with many stars. They include Smokey Robinson, the Neville Brothers, George Thorogood, and the group Blood Sweat & Tears.

Miller has found success as an actor as well, appearing on several Canadian television shows. He was even nominated for a **Gemini Award**, in 2006. Success came early for Miller, but he had to overcome some big personal challenges along the way.

Miller is influenced by soul, blues, and country music. His work has been compared to the music of Eric Clapton, Jeff Beck, and Big Sugar.

Personal Profile

Early Years

Derek Miller, a Mohawk, was born in 1974. He was raised on the Six Nations reserve by his mother after his father died. The reserve is located near the city of Brantford, in southern Ontario.

Growing up on the reserve could be difficult, with some young people feeling that their opportunities were limited. Miller turned to music when he was a teenager. He would often listen to his mother's records and discovered that he loved blues music, especially the music of artists such as Muddy Waters and Stevie Ray Vaughan.

> **"** *Music is a way for me to explore my own Mystery.* **"**

Miller co-hosted the 2009 Canadian Aboriginal Music Awards with Andrea Menard. Together, the duo put on the opening performance of the event.

BORN Derek Miller was born on October 29, 1974, on the Six Nations reserve near Brantford, Ontario.

FAMILY Miller's father died when he was seven. He was raised by his mother.

EDUCATION He attended school on the reserve.

CAREER Miller is a guitarist, singer, and songwriter. He has also acted in several television shows.

Developing Skills

When Miller was 13, his mother gave him a guitar that she had found in his grandfather's closet. Miller loved the guitar and spent hours playing it. He now feels that his grandfather's spirit wanted him to have the old guitar. Miller still writes songs on that guitar today.

Miller spent a great deal of time practising his music. Soon, he was good enough to play in local bands, and he made some records with them. He also began to write songs. In 1999, Miller released his first solo record, *Sketches,* independently. Around the same time, he went on tour with Buffy Sainte-Marie, a well-known Canadian Aboriginal singer. People in Canada took notice of him because of the tour.

A record contract followed, and wider success. In 2002, Miller's album

The closing ceremonies of the 2010 Winter Olympics showcased performances by many Canadian musicians. Miller performed "Let's Have a Party" with Eva Avila and Nikki Yanofsky.

Music Is the Medicine came out. The next year, one of the songs on the album, "Lovesick Blues," won a Juno Award for Aboriginal Recording of the Year.

"Anywhere you go on the reserve, you could throw a rock and hit talent."

The Path to Success

Miller went on tour again. Despite the success he was enjoying with his music, he struggled in his personal life. He had always pushed himself very hard. He became so involved with his career and touring that he began to neglect everything else and did not take care of himself. He became exhausted and dependent on drugs and alcohol. Miller knew he could not continue this way and had to make changes. He took time off from his music career to regain his health and overcome his problems.

In 2006, Miller released the album *The Dirty Looks*, which later received a Juno Award for Aboriginal Recording of the Year. A number of memorable things happened for him in 2010. His next album, called *Derek Miller with Double Trouble*, came out. One of the songs on it was a duet with the well-known country singer Willie Nelson. Recording with Nelson was exciting for Miller. Also, that year Miller sang at the closing ceremonies of the Olympic Games in Vancouver, British Columbia. He performed as well at a jazz festival in New Orleans, Louisiana.

Despite all of his success, Miller has a sense of frustration. He is seen as an Aboriginal Canadian musician, rather than as just a musician. This has made it difficult for him to reach certain audiences. While he is proud to be an Aboriginal Canadian, he also wants to be respected as simply a musician.

Accomplishments

2003 Miller wins his first Juno Award for Aboriginal Recording of the Year. He also wins a Native American Music Award.

2008 He wins his second Juno Award for Aboriginal Recording of the Year for his album *The Dirty Looks*. He also wins two Aboriginal People's Choice Music Awards.

2010 Miller performs at the closing ceremonies of the Winter Olympics in Vancouver, British Columbia.

2011 At the Aboriginal People's Choice Music Awards, Miller wins as Aboriginal Male Entertainer of the Year and Aboriginal Songwriter of the Year.

Throat Singer
Tanya Tagaq

Tanya Tagaq is an Inuit throat singer. Inuit throat singing, or *katajiaq*, is an art form that is traditionally practised by two women who try to see who can last longer. The women attempt to copy sounds heard in nature, such as the sounds of animals or moving ice. They make noises using different parts of the throat and by changing the way they breathe. Tagaq taught herself how to throat sing. She performs by herself instead of with another woman. She has taken this traditional form of music and made it her own.

Personal Profile

Aside from her albums, Tagaq's musical talents can be heard in movies and television shows, including the documentary film *This Land* and the theme song of the CBC show *Arctic Air*.

Early Years

Tanya Tagaq Gillis was born in 1975 in Cambridge Bay, a small town located in the Far North in what later became Nunavut. Her mother, a teacher, is Inuk, and her father is from Great Britain. He moved to Canada to work as an air traffic controller.

Although she loved the beauty of her home and the traditions of the Inuit people, Tagaq found some aspects of life in Cambridge Bay difficult. People in that community must deal with isolation, lack of opportunity,

" . . . my music isn't necessarily solely based on interpreting the land at home. It's also about everybody's experiences. "

and other social problems. Since the community was so small, it had no high school. When she was 15, Tagaq was sent to Yellowknife, Northwest Territories, to attend high school there. After that, she decided to move to Nova Scotia, where she studied art at the Nova Scotia College of Art and Design. Her goal was to become an art teacher.

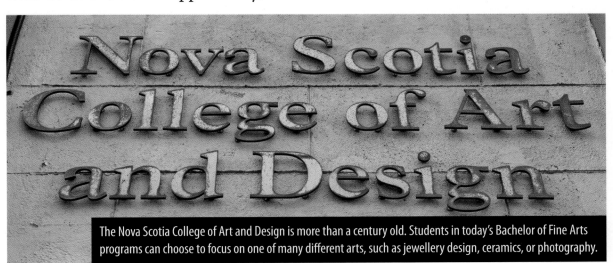

The Nova Scotia College of Art and Design is more than a century old. Students in today's Bachelor of Fine Arts programs can choose to focus on one of many different arts, such as jewellery design, ceramics, or photography.

BORN Tanya Tagaq Gillis was born in 1975 in Cambridge Bay. The town was then in the Northwest Territories but later became part of Nunavut.

FAMILY Tagaq was raised by her parents. She has an older brother and a younger brother. She also has two daughters.

EDUCATION Tagaq attended high school in Yellowknife in the Northwest Territories. She received a Bachelor of Fine Arts degree in 1998 from the Nova Scotia College of Art and Design.

CAREER Tagaq is a singer and painter. She has also worked on short films.

> "Through my music and performances, I hope people can find a healing capacity or joy. I also hope each person takes something different away from my work that they need."

Developing Skills

While Tagaq was at school, she became homesick. To remind her of home, her mother mailed her recordings of women throat singing. Tagaq began to teach herself how to throat sing. She worked to bring her own modern sound to the ancient Inuit art. After a while, she began giving performances. Her style of throat singing quickly

Tagaq is often described as a unique and passionate musician. Most of her performances are improvised, meaning they are not rehearsed or planned out ahead of time.

became popular. Most people had never heard anything like it.

In 2000, Tagaq was showing some of her paintings at an arts festival in Inuvik, Northwest Territories. She also performed at the festival. Two men from Iceland, who were friends of the Icelandic singer Bjork, were in the audience. They told Bjork about Tagaq's unique talent, and Bjork invited Tagaq to go on tour with her in 2001. Tagaq also worked with Bjork on Bjork's album *Medulla* in 2004.

The Path to Success

In 2005, Tagaq released her first album, *Sinaa*. "Sinaa" means "edge" in Inuktitut. That same year, she worked with a musical group called the Kronos Quartet on a piece called "Nunavut," which they performed in Canada, the United States, and Europe. In 2007, she and the Kronos Quartet worked together again, this time on a piece called "Tundra Songs." Tagaq's second album, *Auk/Blood*, came out in 2008.

In 2009, Tagaq helped write and appeared in an award-winning seven-minute film called *Tungijuq*, which was about seal hunting. She also narrated and provided the music for a documentary called *This Land*. *Anuraaqtug*, a live recording of one of her concerts, was released in 2011. More recently, she performed the theme music for the Canadian television show *Arctic Air*.

Tagaq has found success, but she has also received her share of criticism. Some people, especially in the Inuit community, feel that Tagaq is not being true to the traditional art of throat singing. They do not like her modern interpretation of throat singing and feel that she does not respect her heritage and people. Tagaq says that she is introducing throat singing to many people who would never hear it otherwise. She continues to work creatively with many different types of musicians.

Accomplishments

2004 Tagaq performs on Bjork's album *Medulla*.

2005 Tagaq is named Best Female Artist at the Canadian Aboriginal Music Awards. Her album *Sinaa* wins for Best Album Design and Best Producer/Engineer.

2006 *Sinaa* is nominated for a Juno Award for Aboriginal Recording of the Year.

2008 Tagaq's album *Auk/Blood* wins Canadian Aboriginal Music Awards for Best Female Traditional/Cultural Roots Album and Best Album Cover Design.

2009 *Auk/Blood* is nominated for two Juno Awards.

2010 Tagaq performs at the closing ceremonies of the Paralympic Winter Games in British Columbia.

Country Music Singer and Songwriter
Shane Yellowbird

Shane Yellowbird is a country music singer and songwriter. He released hit albums in 2006 and 2009 and has toured across Canada. Yellowbird has won many music awards. Despite his success, singing did not always come easily to Yellowbird. In fact, when he was young, it was even hard for him to speak. Yellowbird had to overcome a serious speech impediment before he could achieve his dream of becoming a country singer.

Early Years

Shane Yellowbird was born in 1979 and raised in the Aboriginal community of Hobbema in central Alberta. He is Cree. He grew up on a ranch, working alongside his family. Ranching can be hard,

In 2007, Yellowbird won the Chevy Rising Star Award at the Canadian Country Music Awards. Besides a trophy, he also received a brand new truck.

Personal Profile

and the family did not always have much money.

In addition to ranching, both of Yellowbird's parents were involved in the rodeo circuit. His mother was a barrel racer, and his father was a calf roper. Yellowbird learned to rope cattle and ride horses when he was very young. When he was older, he also competed in rodeo. He wanted to be a cowboy or a hockey player when he grew up.

" When I think about what I've overcome to make it to where I am right now, it blows me away. I couldn't have done it without the support of the people who are there, watching me on stage every night. "

Yellowbird grew up in the community of Hobbema, Alberta. Local citizens have painted colourful murals of Aboriginal cultural icons on many houses and public buildings in the town.

BORN Shane Yellowbird was born on July 7, 1979, in Hobbema, Alberta.

FAMILY His parents had a ranch. They also competed in rodeos, his mother in barrel racing and his father in calf roping.

EDUCATION Yellowbird has a degree in fine arts from Red Deer College in Alberta. He draws and paints.

CAREER Yellowbird is a country music singer and songwriter.

Developing Skills

When he was young, Yellowbird had a serious stuttering problem. He worked with **speech therapists** to overcome his stutter. A therapist suggested that Yellowbird sing sentences instead of speaking them. Often, people who stutter when they speak do not stutter when they sing. The singing worked and helped Yellowbird with his stutter. He also discovered that he loved to sing.

Yellowbird did not plan to pursue a career as a singer, however. A talented artist, he decided to study for an art degree at a local college. While there, he often went out with his friends to sing **karaoke**. One night, Yellowbird won a karaoke contest. A host at a karaoke club was impressed with his voice and told him he should try to be a professional singer. Yellowbird decided to take a chance and try his luck as a country singer. It was a big dream, but it was something he was passionate about. He also worked hard to write his own songs. These songs were influenced by his love for the cowboy lifestyle as well as the beautiful land in which he grew up.

Yellowbird played against Lanny McDonald in the 2008 Juno Cup. The Cup is a celebrity hockey game between musicians and former National Hockey League players to raise money for a music education charity.

The Path to Success

In 2003, Yellowbird's dream came true when he signed with a **management company** that helped him begin his career. In 2005, his first single, "Beautiful Concept," came out. The next year, his first album was released.

It was called *Life Is Calling My Name* and was a big success. Four songs on the album became top 10 radio hits. *It's About Time*, Yellowbird's second album, came out in 2009. Like his first album, it was very successful.

Accomplishments

2006 Yellowbird wins three awards at the Aboriginal People's Choice Music Awards. He receives Best New Artist, Single of the Year, and Best Music Video.

2007 Yellowbird wins the Chevy Rising Star Award at the Canadian Country Music Awards. At the Aboriginal People's Choice Music Awards, he receives Entertainer of the Year, Best Country Music CD, and Best Music Video. In addition, he takes home three honors at the Canadian Aboriginal Music Awards, for Best Male Artist, Best Country Album, and Album of the Year.

2008 The album *Life Is Calling My Name* is nominated for a Juno Award. At the Aboriginal People's Choice Music Awards, Yellowbird wins Best Music Video.

2009 Yellowbird is honored for Country Recording of the Year at the Native American Music Awards.

2010 Yellowbird performs during the 2010 Winter Olympics in British Columbia. At the Aboriginal People's Choice Music Awards, he wins Male Entertainer of the Year, Single of the Year, and Country Album of the Year. At the Native American Music Awards, he receives the award for Best Country Recording.

Write a Biography

All of the parts of a biography work together to tell the story of a person's life. Find out how these elements combine by writing a biography. Begin by choosing a person whose story fascinates you. You will have to research the person's life by using library books and reliable websites. You can also email the person or write him or her a letter. The person might agree to answer your questions directly.

Use a concept web, such as the one below, to guide you in writing the biography. Answer each of the questions listed using the information you have gathered. Each heading on the concept web will form an important part of the person's story.

Parts of a Biography

Early Life

Where and when was the person born?

What is known about the person's family and friends?

Did the person grow up in unusual circumstances?

Growing Up

Who had the most influence on the person?

Did he or she receive assistance from others?

Did the person have a positive attitude?

Developing Skills

What was the person's education?

What was the person's first job or work experience?

What obstacles did the person overcome?

Person Today

Has the person received awards or recognition for accomplishments?

What is the person's life's work?

How have the person's accomplishments served others?

Early Achievements

What was the person's most important early success?

What processes does this person use in his or her work?

Which of the person's traits were most helpful in his or her work?

Internet Resources

Canadian Aboriginal Music Awards
The official website for the Canadian Aboriginal Music Awards lists all the nominees and winners, as well as the performers at each year's show.

WEBSITE: www.canab.com/mainpages/events/musicawards.html

Native Drums
Native Drums is a website devoted to the heritage of Aboriginal music in Canada. It has games, videos, and much more. Visitors to the site can learn how different Aboriginal drums across Canada are made as well as played.

WEBSITE: www.native-drums.ca

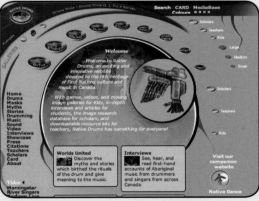

Aboriginal Connections
Aboriginal Connections is a directory of Aboriginal musical talent in Canada. It lists information about each person or group and provides links to official websites. It also lists Aboriginal recording and entertainment companies.

WEBSITE: http://directory.Aboriginalconnections.com/Canada/Arts/Music/index.html

Glossary

Aboriginal: a term that refers to the First Nations, Métis, and Inuit peoples of Canada

activist: a person who works hard for a cause

ancestors: family members who lived in the past

blues: a style of music that was created by African Americans in the southern United States in the early 20th century

chancellor: the honorary head of a university

contract: an agreement between two people or groups that makes it necessary to perform a specific action or actions

Gemini Award: an award presented in Canada for achievements in television

Grammy Awards: awards presented in the United States for achievements in the music industry

Inuk: a person who is a member of the Inuit, a group of people who have traditionally lived in Canada's Arctic regions

Juno Awards: awards presented in Canada for achievements in the music industry

karaoke: a form of entertainment in which people sing into a microphone along with a recorded song

linguist: a person who studies different languages

lyrics: the words of a song

management company: in entertainment, a company that handles the business details of someone's career

Métis: a person who is of mixed Aboriginal and European descent

Mohawk: a First Nations people who are part of the Iroquois Confederacy, an association of several different Aboriginal groups in North America

motivational speaker: someone who makes speeches to inspire an audience

Order of Canada: one of the highest honours given in Canada, to recognize outstanding achievement or service

reserve: land set aside by the federal government for the use and occupancy of a First Nations group

social issues: matters that affect people and that are considered to be problems

soundtracks: the recorded music that accompanies a movie or television show

speech therapists: people who treats speech problems or defects

Index